I Am

Micaela Mone'

I Am

ISBN 9780989173230

On the days that felt like my smile had abandoned me you gave me yours. I will forever love you with all of my art...
Franko, Dallas, and Parker

Acknowledgments

I am grateful that during my labor I was not alone. I am blessed to have so many amazing soul brothers and soul sisters in my life. I cannot thank you enough for your love, encouragement, and talents that you gave unselfishly so that "I Am" could come into existence. Romekia, thank you for always making me beautiful, pushing with me when I was tired, and believing in me. You gave me your flowers at times when I know that you could have used them for your own garden. I love you! Brandi, you have been there since I dreamed from gravel roads. Thank you for your love and support at every show. Stage lights or no lights, thank you. Ashley, you are without a doubt my soul sister. Thank you for loving the Mickey that the world doesn't see. You keep me in check with the truth. I love you. Denise, your words are always on time. Roger, thank you for getting in the trenches and building this dream with me. Mawmaw if I could give you every diamond this earth holds it would still not be enough to thank you. Thank you for showing me what love is. I pray to become the strong loving woman you are. I love you. God connects you with the right souls during your lifetime to grow with you, teach you, love you and even leave you according to His will. I am grateful for the soul experiences I have shared with each of you.

Table of Contents

.

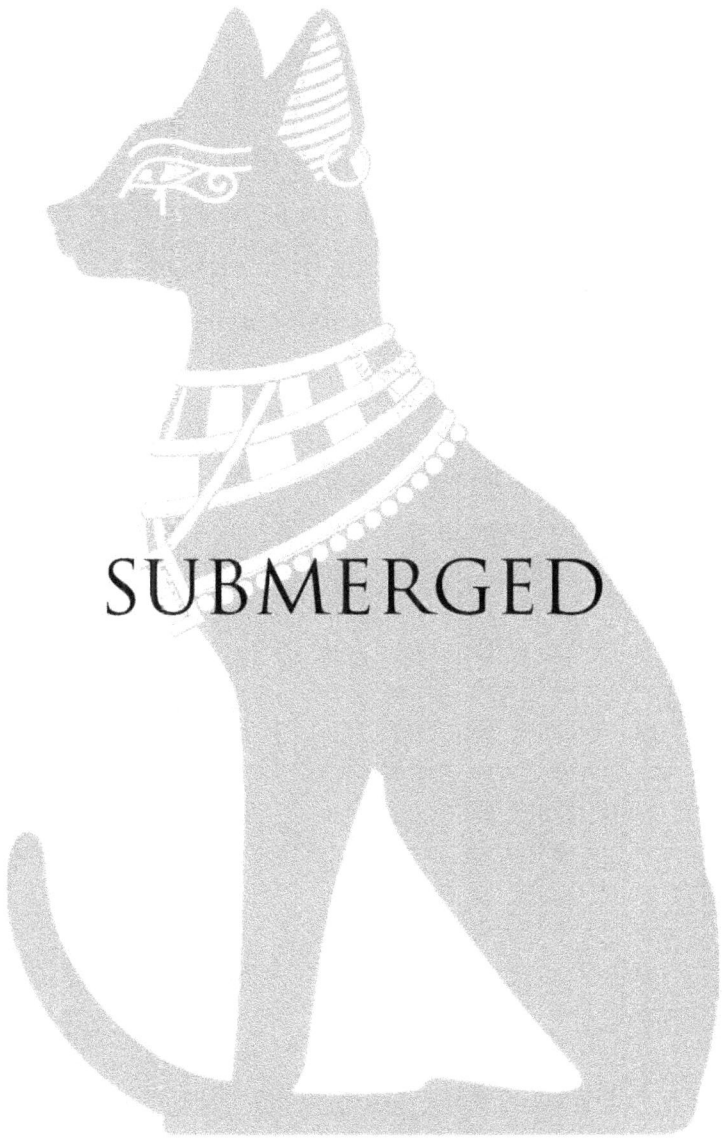

SUBMERGED

Ghost Reflections

She suffers from a past addiction
so she inhales on her past inflictions.
She gets high off of her past decisions.
The damage is so deadly that she's barely living.
Chasing a dragon and running from a ghost.
She never hides because it's the high that she's
needing the most.
Her past is alive and her present is a corpse.
The girl in the mirror has no remorse.
Beware of your past because it can leave you staring at
the reflections of a ghost.

Canton Blues

Their shadows performed nightly outside of my door
Waving back and forth like limbs in a storm
Voices cracking like lightning
Doors slamming like thunder
I remember their lines
My face pressed hard against the wall
Chest filled with air
I was afraid to breathe
I must have been eight or nine when I learned to be
Someone other than me
Digging,
Hiding
places deep within pages
Pulling my hair back becoming
Addy
or
Annie
A slave, an orphan
Believing somewhere someone was looking for me
And I would wait
Until the winds would blow again
Twisters throwing me back and forth

Basement just beneath me, but I never made it off of the
floor
Forced to choose who was right and who was wrong
When I should have been learning the worksheets my
teacher sent home
Throughout all of these years I have carried a broken
child in my poems
Hugging her tightly for all of those times she was alone
Peering into her eyes reassuring her that it is okay to let
go
My notebooks travel to a place and time that has passed
Where only dust remembers I was there
And I sit on a staircase in Ohio
rocking her
Trying to make peace in my soul.

Tag

Did you hear that?
No, no, no, no, listen closely.
Shhhhhhh.... She's crying again.
Can you hear her?
She's crying for someone to come and heal her.
She's waiting for me to save her.
But I don't know if I can face her.

5...... 1,2,3,4,5

Playing hide and seek inside
in the closet that's where she hides
until a hand tags her thigh
and then it slowly slides
up her polka dot dress
But shhhhh.... she's only

1, 2,3,4,5

Damn she's crying again. Can you hear her?
She's crying for someone to heal her
She's waiting for me to go and save her

But I don't know if I can face her.

Still

I seek stillness
One that engulfs a distressed ship before it descends into
nothingness...
Closed eyes; lungs filled
Stillness
Cognizant to the fact that not all breathing beings are
alive
Since living is a process susceptible to changing
And yet some of us remain stagnant
I seek stillness, away from the chatter and trivial
problems
Stillness, my sanctuary to breathe and explore thought
It is there I shall decide

Ten P.M.

As the sun hides
My loneliness rise
Greeted by dark skies
How long does the lonely survive?
One sunset equals a thousand nights
The sentence is always longer for the ones tormented
inside
Conversational thoughts keeps my memories company
so just maybe I'm not really that lonely
But reality is
It takes more than Lysol to cover the smell of shit
I'm in the need of learning the art of forget
I've tried to forgive
But as long as I can remember it seems as if the pain I
relive
Don't mind me I'm just rambling how I feel
It's 10pm again

Hieroglyphics

No tattoos because upon my wrists I bear Egyptian tombs
Hieroglyphics meaning the Queen shall rise soon
Talitha Cumi
I rise even when weak
Ancient battles
Depression so moist on my chest it rattles
But I still breathe
Inhaling deep when I smile so when shadows arise I can
remember
The breath of joy
A fire will start as long as I can reflect on the pieces inside
of me that ember
This is why when I laugh, I laugh loud until it echoes
inside of my soul
Until it fills every part of me that this life has made cold
Until I forget for a spell
No tears, no hurt
I am grateful for the moments when I can just live
My skin has no tattoos, but my walls are filled

PTSD

She's never been deployed
But she's been to war
Never worn fatigues
But she's prayed for relief
Frontlines have left her with the belief
That love is a battle so she refuses to be seized
Shell shocked
As long as she's armed she'll never believe
Shell shocked
Still firing after all fighting has ceased
Shell shocked
Somebody please tell her it's okay to breathe

Edna

As the world she rose daily with slept, she crept from
the place she laid and awakened her soul in thought.
Deep within the recesses of her mind she was alive.
Nightly she would visit her sanctuary disrobing the cloths
that hid her. And there she would dance. Away from
judgment she explored her own truths and tasted each
one carefully. Picking them from branches; some of them
almost sweeping the ground like her grandmother's
broom from the fruit it bore. Each truth possessing a
robust taste. And like a ritual she ate the same truth last
every night. Small truth painting her palate with the
same sour sweetness as a kumquat. She would partake it
whole, swallowing seeds and all. Then without haste she
would prune her tree by burning the dead and fruitless
branches. Right before her departure she would bathe.
And it was there one night as she soaked in the oils of her
desires that she discovered she was Edna. Two souls
separated by 115 years. Alone she cried. Tears falling and
coupling until she labored her own Pontchartrain. In-
stead of swimming out into the vast abyss of her pain she
rose above it like storm clouds hovering over a tumescent
lake and she inhaled. She inhaled deeply evaporating all

that she cried until she could precipitate again because the sun would be rising soon. She and Edna would have to wait until another day to be awakened and finally set free.

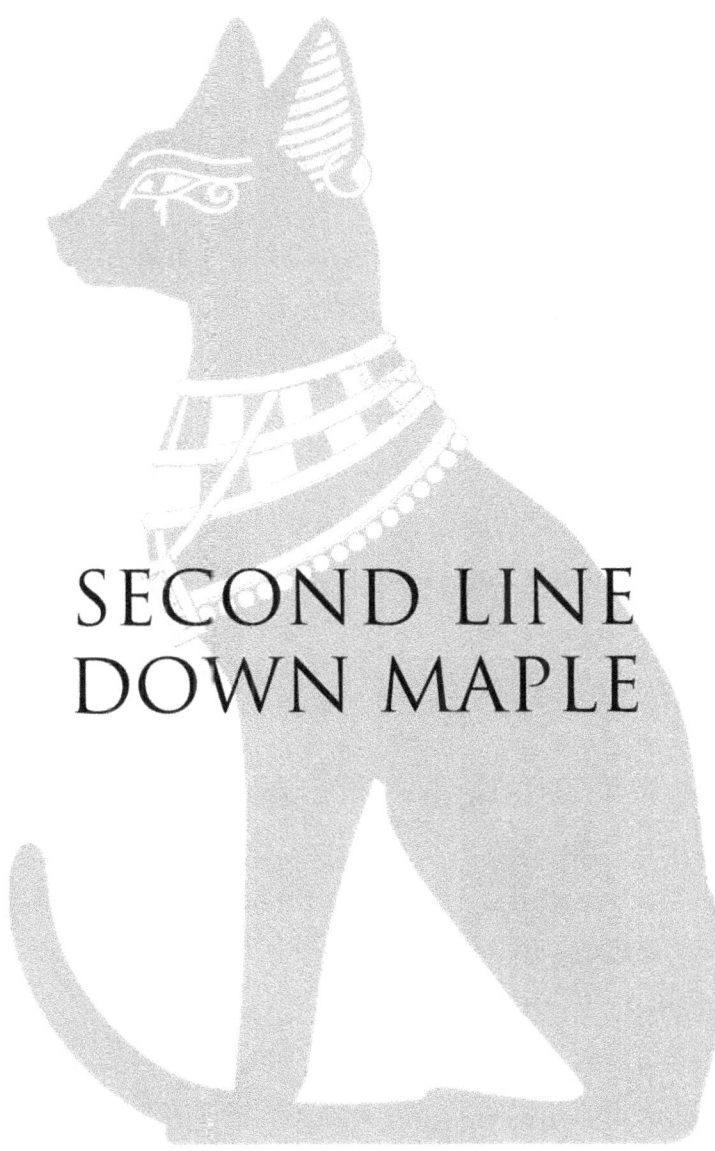

SECOND LINE
DOWN MAPLE

Olive Tree

I hated her
Cursed the gametes that created her
So lost in his lies I couldn't see that the boat I was riding
in was the same as her
Foolishly competing; we crowned him King
And he didn't even have a throne to rule from
Just a delusional soul wandering the earth on a quest to
conceive sons
Playing Kingdom
Basking in his ability to condition his pawns to be broken
 We were his faithful servants
Honored to be on set even if it was the backside of his
curtains
Hurting
Trying to be his better best only opened ourselves for the
pain to worsen
Now I find myself trying to outrun his shadows in the
hopes of losing that person
That I have so shamelessly become
Reflecting and re-reflecting searching for a way to make
this pain undone

All that we do no matter how indecorous becomes our
legacy

Above all else I'm a mother so it matters how my babies
look at me

So before I go any further I have some repenting to do

Pontius Pilate my hands in holy water "Forgive us father
for we know not what we do"

6,909 miles away from Israel, we must be the descend-
ants of one of Jacob's sons

Because we are a lost generation shepherd by only our
wants

And I'm just trying to make sense of where I'm going

Close the gate to where I've been because dead grounds
deserve no sowing

But my reflection won't let me escape without reminding
me of my faults

It is your eyes that I see every time my mirror fogs

How can I proclaim to be my sister's keeper when pride
has kept me from making peace?

How can I empower women to wear their crowns without
crowning all of our Queens?

And Queen I bow to you placing apologies at your feet

Purging hate from my heart in hopes that all strife will
flee

Placing forgiveness over the transgressions that I believed
you had done unto me
And Queen you must know
Your worth is more valuable than all of the gold that this
Earth holds
Your crown is welded to your soul
By birth right you have inherited sovereign control
You never have to relinquish your title in the name of love
You never have to share the throne with anyone other
than your King and the Man above
And please Queen whatever you do, never answer to a
name other than the one your mother gave you
Your babies are watching so never give any man walking
the power to rate you
Love lives in you
Allow it to cover your wounds and heal you
An army of a 100,000 fills you
A higher power lifts you
So do not be dismayed
Deafen your ears to lies that want you to believe your
King is not on his way
Life is just beginning so never stop reaching
Impossible is merely a word created by those who can
never repair their souls from breeching

I Am

Forgive me if I'm preaching
But these are words that I should have long ago shared
with you
Who better to know your pain than someone who once
bared it too
Heavier was my load because I carried stones of
indignation
I breathe easier now because it's truth and not lies that
I'm embracing
I had to take my crown back in order to stop running and
start facing
That our tears came from the same well
And we were both blindly waiting
Dying of thirst convinced somehow that this was Jacob's
well
Volunteering ourselves to be subjected to the wrath of a
broken man's hell
Queen I just pray that after all of this you understand
I come to you only after searching every corner, even
crevice of this land
Weeping at its roots until I knew I could not take just the
branch
 I had no choice but to uproot the whole tree
Because if ever I hate my sister in truth I hate me.

17

Micaela Mone'

Collateral Damage

He was lusting after lust
stronger than any bust that he could ever feel
And I was just collateral damage on his battlefield
Unarmed
And yet I was harmed
I must have been not only blind, but deaf to miss the
alarms
Love offering in my arms
Walking upon
a land of a million bombs.
Intoxicated by his lips I impetuously marched on
Never awakening to the sounds of collapsing homes.
No, love is not a battlefield
But lust is an enemy that shoots to kill.

Baptisms in Amsterdam

He has a ritual of baptizing his ghosts in gin.
Making them disappear for a moment, but by morning
they're back again.
10 am and he's drinking.
Face etched in regret because he's thinking.
Every face reminds him of her.

Micaela Mone'

Bathroom Confessionals

Yes I'm still hurt;

I won't hide it or try to lie.

You cracked me in the deepest place of my soul.

I do my best but the pain at times leaves me nauseous.

Hate has consumed me

Strong because it is rooted from my cracks;

the cracks deep within me.

I have changed and inevitably become the thing I most despise.

I can only pray for time.

Time heals all wounds.

I need time to learn forgiveness.

Like David

I cry the tears that he won't even cry for himself

Shaking from the grief that the last one left

Salt and pain leaves a bad aftertaste

But bottles of vodka makes it all go away

Followed by bad hangovers filled with the problems of yesterday

He writes daily obituaries as he buries his problems away

Exchanging sorrow for orgasms, another girl another day

And I cry for him because I know he hurts

But it's impossible to save someone without them wanting to be saved first

But yet I fight for him

Because inside of him beats the heart of David therefore inside of him is the heart of God

He too can slay giants if only he knew how much greater is He on the inside

And I pray that God gives him new eyes

So that he may see its day instead of midnight

He's a step away from victory if he'll let go of defeat

I'm on my knees praying like I'm his mama that he'll open his eyes and see

There will never be a more woeful sight than a man with
broken wings
And I pray.

Wilderness of Sin

Have you ever been so consumed by someone else's
shadow?
Tried running in all four directions but never really able
to travel
far enough to break out of their blackness
The stigma of their filth fuels all madness
Bleaching of skin, scrapping of flesh
Up all night
Thine eyes know not of rest
Torturous habits
Comparable to a Meth addict
I do not snort, smoke, or inject
But I do need help
Point me to the fences of this concentration camp
My concentration's stamped
By the wrath
of the lack
of his love.
Miles upon miles I am running
Free,
But in need
to escape his borders.

In the pitch black of night his branches are snapping back
against my skin
I am wounded
But I cannot stop moving.
There is water outside the Wilderness of Sin.

Declaration

Nine, like a cat with nine lives

Years, like Jodie doing his bid

Time is constant, but always changing

And I'm,

I'm still here.

Here.

Yes, over the years I've mastered the art of pushing good

men away and chasing dogs

And since dogs eat shit

I've acquired the palate and now it's my main dish

I guess you become accustomed to crawling once you

answer to bitch

I'm tired

Tired like Ol Yeller except this is no movie set

Tired because all I ever wanted was a lover and not these

regrets

Tired because I gave away all of me and now only a dog is

left

Yep I'm tired of eating shit so if you see the old me tell

her I'm looking for myself

Wait....

Cancel that

I'm better than that

I wrote those lines last week

When I was knocking my wooden floor with bended
knees

Choking on tears you get the picture you know how
misery be

Terry McMillan hit close to home when she penned
Bernadine

Now, that was my favorite scene

Now I know what it means

To finally exhale

Thought I was drowning lungs burning and then I
inhaled

You tried to sink me, but I caught my second wind

Just for you I took my heels off, but "patna" I'm still a
GIANT

And understand this well I could be penniless, holding
my three babies, standing barefoot in the slums of
Kingston and still be QUEEN!

So don't think for just a second I'm taking my crown off

What did I say earlier?

 I was looking for myself

The Queen is back so next time you come around brother you better humble yourself!

Heads of Bull

Be leery of a man with an insatiable appetite because he
will never be satisfied
No, he is like a bottomless well inside.
He knows no end.
He will drink of you and drink of them
Drink of many until they're all weak from him
Oh, bewildered woman, foolish is she that stands in the
path of destruction
And curtails the innocence of her children's childhood in
the name of trusting
A man without reason
One that enjoys feasting
But never becomes full
Be leery of those lovers that wear the heads of bulls

Weekend Lover

She said he only loves her on the weekend
Weeping
Only when it's convenient
Fleeting
Time is precious but he's not seeing

So the battle song plays

She tells me to look at her and I cannot even deny her
beauty
Love like that should never be a duty
And yet she is alone
Familiar with only the tone
Of his voice and not his arms
Forever she mourns

So the battle song plays

She's crying oh weekend lover
Why can't you see its easier to love her
Oh weekend lover

First heartbreak was her father.
First heartbreak was her father.

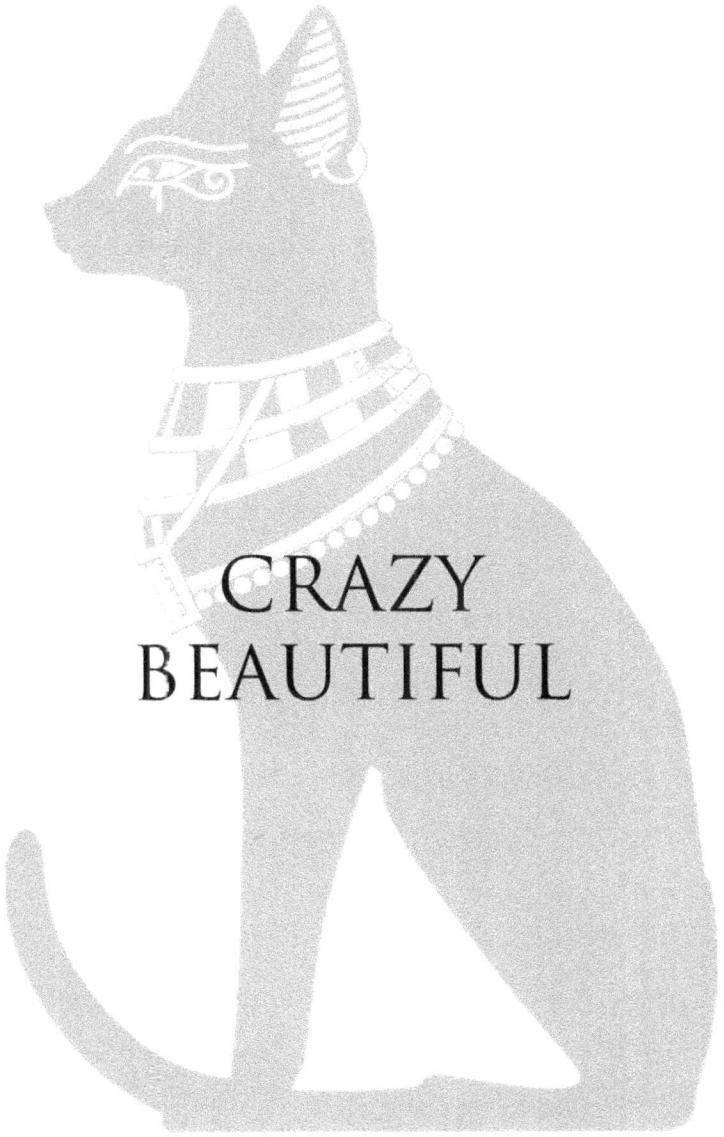

CRAZY
BEAUTIFUL

Crazy Beautiful

Crazy beautiful
You're beautiful until it's crazy
There's so much hate in this world
But don't let it break you, baby girl
They said that you were crazy, but you are really more
than beautiful

6:45 her alarm goes off she awakens to see she was
dreaming
Her head hits her pillow again as she fights to find a
reason
To get up and go to a place where the devil himself was
breathing
Water splashes her face
Mirror echoes back yesterday
When rumors spread like fire how are you suppose to
fight back
High school hallways should never be like Iraq
And yet every day they were coming back strapped
Phone and inboxes blowing up as if she had been hacked
Silently she cried
Couldn't fathom telling her parents why

Lately dressing and leaving without good byes

Breakfast uneaten; she was slowly being defeated by lies

Her spirit weakened, but refusing to die

Crazy beautiful

You're beautiful until it's crazy

There's so much hate in this world

But don't let it break you, baby girl

They said that you're crazy, but you are really more than
beautiful

11:45 the bell rings

It's time to switch again

She gets up

Picks her books up

But they're knocked back down again

Her ears ring with their laughing

Her mouth is dry and she feels like choking

Her legs want to run, but her feet feel swollen

So she stands there as they walk away snickering

Chained in place by the words they say; her light keeps
flickering

After a moment her feet become lighter and she darts
outside

Moving swiftly cursing the tears that fall from her eyes
Why doesn't anyone notice her grief?
She's an angel walking through hell's hallway with invisible wings

Crazy beautiful
You're beautiful until it's crazy
There's so much hate in this world
But don't let it break you, baby girl
They said that you're crazy, but you're really more than beautiful

2:55 the last bell rings for the day
She turns the corner; her eyes crash into his face
Then it all replays
Every text, call, kiss, and whisper holding her at bay
He use to be perfect; everything she dreamed of
She just wanted to feel special so naively she gave him her love
All Star Athlete
Misfit geek
This time Cinderella wouldn't be queen
Slipper left broken because everything is never as it seems

Innocence captured on video shared with the team
Spread out like wildfire, savaging anything left in her
garden that was green
If anything he was the one that should be paying
As their eyes met his laughs became silenced by the pleas
her eyes were saying

Crazy beautiful
You're beautiful until it's crazy
There's so much hate in this world
But don't let it break you, baby girl
They said that you were crazy, but you are really more
than beautiful

6:45 alarm
7:00 alarm
7:15 alarm
"Baby are you getting ready in there?"
7:25 her mother finds her sleeping
Only this time she will not depart from her dreaming
Her mother frantically shakes her body that has turned
cold
7:47 the bell rings as her parents discover her last note
Please forgive me, but I couldn't bare hell anymore

Altar Call

I write poetry because I know there's a Mickey out there
who has been to the altar a thousand times
Dropped to her knees crying loud
Praying that Jesus may heal her mind
And after the altar call is finished she walks outside
Gets into her ride and proceeds to drive
And before she leaves the lot sadness again fills her eyes
I am not claiming to have all of the answers, but I do
know that after every dark night the sun does rise
And even if the devil throws grenades inside of your mind
Hold on just a little bit longer because sometimes victory
takes time
Front lines can be disheartening
Memories have a way of distorting
Our perspectives of life
That's why even when you can't see it you must fight
harder to feel the light
Seeds begin in darkness before they ever reach their
highest height.

Nefertiti

The beautiful one has come so I call her Nefertiti
I steal her broken mirror in hopes that she will answer
thee
From her throne she cries a river praying to drown her
past
From her eyes to the Mediterranean Sea grasping at the
moments that never last
I see her not as she sees herself
A Queen that will be loved not one that love has left
Nefertiti stand!
You have conquered battles in ancient lands
As the wind blows from your pain I can hear them still
praising your name
The beautiful one has come
The beautiful one is here
Nefertiti stand and be
You were born a Queen dry your tears and you will see
Nefertiti.

Parker

Even though I know I physically cannot hold you forever
it doesn't stop me from wanting to.
Even though I know the disappointments of life are
unstoppable I want to stand in between you and them.
If I could I would give you sunshine and laughter every-
day
But I cannot so instead I promise to always wipe the tears
from your face.
Every night I will pray for you.
Nothing will ever change the love I have for you.
Dreams I have for you, but I want nothing more than for
you to have dreams too.
And if no one else can see your vision I will see it with
you.
So many things I want to give to you.
Like kindness, love, patience, hope, encouragement.... I
want you to be better than me.
I pray I never teach you my flaws
Instead I pray that you learn from them and be better
Parker, this is my love letter....

Soap box

As of lately my vestibulocochlear nerve anticipates
transmitting auditory information from my ears to my
brain which then translates
A puzzled stranger, friend, new acquaintance inquisition
as to why I am still single
You see, pretty girls aren't suppose to be single

On the daily, social networks tell me I am beautiful
Notifications blowing up but I don't post pics like the
usual
I was once told that I did not post enough body shots
That my lack of selfies had them wondering what I was
really about
But daily I post thoughts
Literally more naked than their favorite porn star
I would much rather be known as deep than pretty
And yet, I'm too pretty to be single is all they see

That foolery is an insult

For years bombing away at me

Until at 26 I'm up pass midnight questioning the same
thing to me
While my three kids are in their rooms tucked fast to
sleep

I am single

Single because I once betted all on a love that was never
meant for me
Broken from years of loving too much and never having
that love reciprocated to me
It's been over ten years since I won my last pageant, but
for him I would compete
Always trying to outdo the last chick, but I stayed with a
losing streak
The same way you beat a slave down is how you make a
woman weak

I am single.

Because I chose a delivery room instead of an abortion
room
No fairy tales ever told me you could end up with a baby
daddy instead of a groom

And now I am racing against time because the hours are
never on my side
For a paper that says degree to better their lives
I won't front like I don't know what they really need is a
father by their side

I am single.

Single because I am still trying to find the E in love that
my father never taught.
E as in encouragement
Enthusiasm when I brought back good grades
E as in eternity because love never fades
E as in embarking, engaging, enlightening, educating,
embracing and elevating
I have found out that love without E is only mating
I am single because now I know my worth
And as confusing as it may seem to you I now put myself
first
And refuse to settle all in the name of a pretty picture
painted inside of your head
So yes, I am single
I am pretty
But I would much rather you know me as deep

Ashes for Beauty

Ashes for beauty
So I tore each page and set them afire
Ashes for beauty
Their footprints leave no warning; our daughters are
trudging a path that leads them into deep mire
Ashes for beauty
I am guilty of arson
For I have ripped the pages from the hands of brothers
And burned every fable, every fairytale while repenting
the sins of past mothers
I will not read my daughter fairytales
She will not be tucked in to sleep upon feather stuffed
pillows and white lies
Nor will she be sang prince charming lullabies
Poison the masses if you may, but my daughter shall be
wise
While the other damsels will wait in distress, my daugh-
ter, she will rise
I will not feed her lines inked in the 1600's by the hands
of dead men preconditioning her to believe that she is
feeble
Planting seeds of desire to be saved

Are we so blinded that we have yet to see where the
mystical woods lead to?
The "Once upon a time" and "far, far away" beautiful
maiden has for years made our daughters superficial
Golden locks and flowing hair we willingly predispose
them to a beauty that's fictional
"Who is the fairest of them all?"
Twenty something year old battling the images reflected
back from the mirror hanging on the wall
It is just glass.
All of it glass.
Even she is glass.
Breakable by any stone
Because it is well pass 12 and now she searches for a
Prince to bring her home
Frantically trying to write a fairytale of her own
But her pages are filled
With the ink she has spilled
Sleepless nights she encounters because she craves for a
love that isn't real
Her mother read of happy endings, but never of a heart
that wouldn't heal
And time is selfish
And she is helpless

Micaela Mone'

I will never read my daughter a fairytale
Because I know of too many women who have chased line
after line losing themselves along the trail

Lupita

I am from a place where people are quick to embrace
their Creole heritage and bleach the Negro from their face
Pay hundreds of dollars for DNA testing to find out they
trace back to Africa any damn way
I am from a place where my great-great grandmother
would have referred to me as "negress" had she seen me
after my "color came in"
Backwoods, paper bag tests, small teeth combs
God forbid you were light skin with nappy roots showing
It's funny how self hate is a generational crop that keeps
on growing
But like Ms. Sophia say "Dere is a God"
And he showed up at the Oscars last night
Black and beautiful
Caused a stirring in souls
Unashamed letting her roots show
And to think she was once a little black girl that hated
herself
From a place where people would bleach their skin
because beauty was taught by someone else
Dear sisters I love your black
Our midnight, caramel, cocoa bean black

Pecan colored like candy in my grandmother's kitchen
black
Louisiana soil black
Desert black
Smooth like oil in Arabia black
Your beauty surpasses the melanin in your skin
It's your soul my sister where the beauty begins
So never hide yourself away and never stop dreaming

Soul Warrior

Our universe is filled with noise, constant noise, but I
heard you speak
It was barely a whisper
Sometimes the whispers are the loudest things
Somewhere in between the jokes and laughter, when no
one was looking, your soul spoke to me
"Soldiers get weak"
Three words that darted at me like a lightning bolt,
hitting my soul leaving me paralyzed
Focusing me past your laughter and adjusting my vision
to your eyes
I see you
I see the mighty spirit tucked inside
Carrying the girl that sometimes cry
the woman that is sometimes tired
I saw the place where you quietly grieve
the corners where you lift your windows to allow your
soul to breathe
It was there that I read you
All of the thoughts that you never wrote
Words that had filled your mouth, but you never spoke

Brick walls surrounding regrets, heartbreaks, and
emptiness
Uncertainties, failures, and secrets
But there was a light in you
Lit daily by God himself flaming the fight in you
Drying those tears when no one else was near
And rocking the child because no matter how old we grow
we are His still
And peace is His will
Soldiers get weak, but rest well knowing that your Father
does heal
I saw you
The beautiful beyond your flawless skin
The perfection beyond your smile
More divine than Cleopatra
I heard your war cry
and it sung to me, lifting me to my feet
Warming my soul with your joys and laughter, blanketing
me in your victories
Sweet victories
Because every day that you arise despite any storm inside
Is a victory
Every face that you plant a smile
Is a victory

And I thank you

I love you

If ever your mirror doesn't show you this reflection

Look at the children and you will see

You have love, you have joy, and you have peace.

Tim McGraw

With eyes closed I can see you and you look like my
poetry.
Faithfully I read you like my grandmother praying her
rosary
And this is what love feels like
A breath of air filling drowning lungs
A ray of light after a long dark storm
Love is a reviving thing
And that's the sound of my heart beating again
I'm staring at you and you look like my poetry
Deep and beautiful... Just like my words you are a part of
my story
Love is a reviving thing

Imagine Love

Imagine for a second that you have a rare diamond
in your possession. Never mind how you acquired it
because life has a way of giving and taking things we are
worthy and unworthy of. Now imagine your excitement
over this diamond....the beauty and rarity of it. How
would you feel if you were notified that the rare diamond
that you possessed was a mere decoy diamond. The
excitement you once had now dissipates, shame follows,
and you no longer value the beautiful stone. The rare
diamond may have been fallacious but it's beauty was still
undeniable. The same applies to people we encounter in
life. When we begin to explore and discover half-truths
buried just beneath their surface we become oppressed by
our feelings. We allow the pictures in our heads to dictate
to us how someone else should be. The magic disappears,
the experience becomes false and we walk away from the
beauty of it all. We are addicts of euphoria. As beautiful
as it is even a sunset is an illusion

You Are Powerful

"You are meant to have an AMAZING life." -Rhonda Byrne

The above quote is not limited to a certain group of people, it speaks to everyone. Every person that walks this earth deserves an amazing life and can live one. Everyone possesses the power to do so, but very few are aware of their power. On the other hand, many of us simply do not know how to use this power.

We are in a constant state of expectancy. What you expect directly affects what you receive. Be cautious of becoming preconditioned to subpar results. Many times people allow bad relationships, failures, shame, guilt, etc to fester inside of them. Carrying such loads predisposes them to accept and expect them again. If you are expecting something you tend to seek it. What you seek you will find. Before you start each day self check your soul. At the end of each night unload your baggage. Expect happiness, love, success, life abundantly..... inhale it and it will manifest. Allow it to light your soul. The greatest power we have is often the biggest secret.... Love. Love for self, love for others... love is so powerful and yet so unused.

"Take away love and our earth is a tomb." -Robert Browning

Yes, you were created to have an amazing life. Do not wait any longer to live in happiness and in love.

Collector's Item

By human nature we are collectors. Throughout our entire lives we are collecting and in search for more. We are collectors of moments... we collect our successes and failures, disappointments and blessings, lies and truths, hurts and pleasures, loves and hates...we collect time, memories, people and lessons. Then when we study our collection instead of seeing a masterpiece in progress we only see our fragments. We dwell upon missing lessons or experiences that we should have lived.... could haves, should haves and secretly we search to fill our empty shelves and mend our broken places. We are collectors by nature, imperfect by default, but nevertheless beautiful.

Favor

The odds are in your favor. No matter what you are going through, no matter how hard you hit the bottom, no matter how far you have left to go, or how big the mountain is the odds are in your favor. You are the winning the number. Out of the approximate 400 possible eggs and 100,000,000 plus sperm you were conceived. Not only were you conceived, but you are here. If you are reading this it means you have beat many other odds along the way. The odds are in your favor. What you do with that favor depends solely on you.

Micaela Mone'

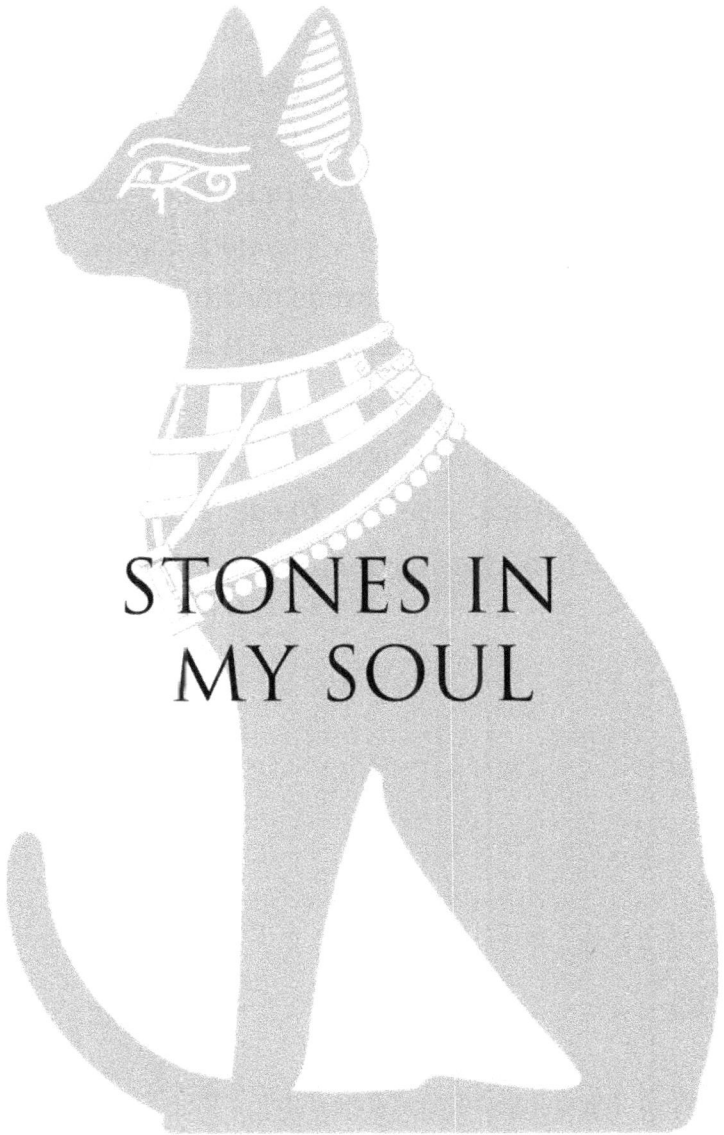

STONES IN
MY SOUL

Through my pen I become them.
I become the misfit, the misunderstood, the misfortu-
nate. I become the outcast, the struck down, the forgot-
ten. I feel the pain of the lady that wanders aimlessly on
the street. I wear my father's combat boots and shed
post traumatic tears. I become the little girl that fears
the hands of men more than monsters. Nightly I rock
her to sleep. Through my pen I become the bullied. The
boy who walks hallways crushed by the word fag. I
bear his burden. I become the girl that covers her
wrists; the man chasing a setting sun. I become them.

Black Swan

Size seven heels permanently imprinted into the edges of
her embankment
For years she made a weekly hajj to her personal Mecca
ridding herself of the stones she kept stored, stacked to
her ceiling
Her mother's scarf always covered her head as she
watched the water ripple
Since she was five it had been her ritual
A sort of dumping place
Because too many stones impaired her pace
And they were always mounting inside
No matter how beautiful her dresses and bows were, to
her they were just nice
Somebody must have told her... someone planted a seed
Conditioning her to believe
Roots spreading to her eyes teaching them to see
A reflection distorted
Girl disturbed desperately trying to restore it
En Pointe and leaps
Bourree across the floor, she would spin until her feet
would bleed
Swan Lake

Perfection was better than great

So many times she was on top and didn't know

Preoccupied with proving she was good enough left her in pursuit of more

Seasons continually changed

But her state of consciousness stayed the same

Stones escorting her across a University's stage

Weighing her fingertips down every time she updated her page

By spring time her wings were glorious, she had completely bloomed

The girls she desired to be like were now like forgotten decor in the room

For once it seemed as if the curse was broken

Her trips to Mecca became less frequent the more she believed she was awoken

Designer bags now carried her stones so she had no need for unloading

Network followers became her audience so she kept uploading

Pride crept upon her while she was distracted by her appearance

Vanity arrived in broad daylight stealing her deliverance

No matter how many degrees you obtain you are still

I Am

susceptible to ignorance

Whoever success doesn't humble it controls

And it had her walking sleeveless with black wings in the

brunt of winter unaware that it was cold

My only hope is that she'll journey back before

succumbing to her load

Beauty is much more than merely being beautiful

Poster Girl

It's been said forever
that mama always knows better
Too bad she couldn't remember
mama's words the day trouble met her
All senses failed her
His smiled weakened her defenses; lust wouldn't let her
Recognize him as danger......

She fell in love with a stranger and never knew it
Baby girl 17 and a whole lot of foolish
Blinded by conversations and compliments
In her eyes gifts and rides were welcoming
Passenger side baby that's what you call entitlement
Now she's wondering where her title went
Locked away into a room where no lights come in
Prince Charming is gone, her price tag he's pocketing

Mama always knows better
Too bad we never find out until after worst weather

Her dear mama sitting at the table
Grandmother standing by her side praying she'll be able

To stay strong
Holding a picture begging the detectives to bring her
baby back home
It's been days.... countless calls, text messages..... she
knew something was wrong
"Somebody has my baby they turned off her phone"
The detective nods, asks more questions, writes more
notes
Who was the last to see her? Describe her clothes.

The room is somber everyone's worst fear sits heavily
upon their throats
Impossible to swallow; even harder to breathe
Young girls if you're listening you better take heed
The old folks always know better, that you better believe

While she works
They search
She's died a thousand deaths
Her face on every corner her mother never rests

Printing missing posters, her friends are besides them-
selves

Racking themselves with guilt because they should have
been there to help

And while they look
She's booked
Numbed no longer shook
Present in body but her mind is flying to a place where
she is free
She no longer feels. Occasionally she reminds herself to
breathe.

She's our poster girl, up on every corner
She's just another number
11.4 million to be exact
32 billion dollar industry and yet she hasn't seen one
check

And today we met

I saw her smiling from a missing poster
Truth be told she's not far she's really much closer
Seventeen but she feels much older
This isn't the life she chose it's the one that chose her
Confined in a room filled with prayers

You might mistake it for holy grounds if it weren't for the
nightmares

And monsters

Quite often men that walk amongst us

Predators wearing masks

Who take their sinful ways and cast

Them into the souls of young girls

This is our dirty secret in a bleached out world

She's waiting

They're waiting

Praying to be found

Just another girl on a poster

Replaying the words that her mother once told her.

Ruptured Eardrums

The truth hurts so we resort to whispering
Veiled eyes can't protect our tympanic membrane from
blistering
The needles on the record and it's this again
I'm from a place where young girls throw their futures
away
in hopes of exchanging climaxes for love this is how they
lay
In search of a feeling
Desperately trying to fill the emptiness their father's left
It's a dog eat dog world now our daughters hate them-
selves
Sentencing themselves to the swipes of Snap cards
A four digit code providing these babies with limitless
snack bars
Wic offices disguised as governmental help
But in actuality a tomb of thoughts wondering outside of
themselves
The could of, should of, would of been thoughts
Walls soaked in bitterness, wet in touch
Reject and failure have become their crutch

And because no one tells them better they're convinced that this is life.

WENDY

She says she's so tired of eulogies
"I've cried my heart out so many times it's nothing new to
me."
Cue the choir please
So many flowers mixed with sniffling, but she ain't got no
allergies
No, that's how Wendy grieves
Because one weekend it was five the other weekend it was
eight.
"I'm forced to bury these babies who have no concept of
hate."
Stray bullets with agendas to kill, but no paths to take
Usually finds its final destination in whoever stands in
the way
Leaving Wendy with tears forever stained on her face
Wendy told me 48 wounded in a weekend is the norm for
her
Cursing the manufacturers that keep harming her
She told A&E to keep their 48 hours because it wasn't
long enough
She's convinced the others have forgotten her

Too busy with oval offices to notice what's been rocking
her
Maybe they're just too blinded by the rap deals and "all of
the lights"
But I guess that's what money does when the price is
right
I've never seen Wendy standing needy with her hands
stretched out
But I've seen her knees bloody from prayers her soul has
stressed out
She keeps a bottle of oil because she constantly lays
hands
Trying to rid her sons of ghosts, afraid that they will
become the next man
When Wendy speaks I listen close because of the wisdom
she holds
She said in the Chi when the wind blows it cuts you
straight to your soul
It cuts you straight to your soul
It cuts you straight to your soul.

Opaque

Much too rare to be referred to as a pronoun so I won't
call her she
or even use queen
when referring to her entity.
I have learned to let just be.
Opaque to the rest of the world, but transparent to me.
I see.
Fluently speaking a language that no one else can speak.
I breathe
with the same heavy chest
that protects
a sinful, but forever repenting heart beat.
Opaque
And yet I read.
There is beauty in your mystery.
You are stronger than you believe.
Opaque,
the sun can only reach that which is open to receive.
It's safe to open your window
I'll sit with you whenever your soul needs to breathe.

Giselle

I have searched for you

But you are spread across a million frames

Yesterday I became worried because too many names

succumb to fame

You must be hidden in a space between some lyric and

the stage

Where you can hum somebody else's song and press your

skin against your daughter's face

Artist

Regardless

If they're creating with paints or notes

Performing lines or writing quotes

Give unselfishly of themselves

Born with naked souls

they are exposed

To feeling the cries and woes of everyone else

The artist is a window

Who soul sits at its bay waiting for the sun and the re-

freshing that comes whenever the wind blows

Opened to inspirations

Constantly evolving both for and from creations

Molded within the womb to be givers

Strengthened by their journeys to be lifters

And this is why I have searched for you.

The woes of one man's soul alone can be bearing let alone the weight of this world

Fame takes art and perfects it, refusing to accept anything less

Paints even the artist

I can't help but to wonder how many can still recognize themselves.... After the paint is washed away how much of them are really left.

After every record is broken and ceiling bust open what is really next

After your eyes have seen every shade that this earth can bare

And every place that you have ever wanted to visit you have slept and awoken many times there

After you have performed on all of the world's stages

And sat amongst the most influential graces

I pray

That Giselle saved enough of her away to love for herself

A Father's Love

A Georgia sky ripped open
An Alabama sky torn apart
A Texas sky pried unlock
An Arkansas sky pulled back
A Mississippi sky dragged on its knees
An Alabama sky slit wide
A Florida sky peeled raw
Both North and South Carolina skies stripped bare
A Virginia sky pierced into
and a Louisiana sky cracked and crippled
By the wails
By the howls
Of a soul grieving
A man in despair
Tortured by his own sight
Chained mentally because he knew better than to fight
Soul splitting, departing with his kids and wife
This may very well be their burial because they will never
reunite
The weeping of a slave
Was so intense it still echoes today
If only we would mute our static

The soul of a man born into chains

Could reach beyond fields until he was striking the skies

above beckoning them to rain

If only we could mute our static

The love of a father, whose name was nigger more times

than his own, would not die in Confederacy

His love would travel to his children's sides, covering

them and escaping slavery

If only we could mute our static

Because we are astray in the oblivion of our frequencies

An era of baby mamas/ baby daddies has collapsed the

order of the way things should be

So instead of a weeping slave

Our society is filled largely with men that walk away

Some of them will even pay

$400 plus dollars to tell them they're the pappy, look at

the paper and not even stay

5 minutes to look into their son's eyes

Conscience free men sleep well every night

Some say God is a woman, but if she was she would haunt

them with their baby's cries

Plague them with the mother's woes

It would be like old Egypt minus Pharaoh

I Am

Because a man that denies his flesh isn't worthy of any
crown
I know of a man that burns his chest because he constant-
ly drinks it down
No diapers, no wipes, no clothes, socks, or shoes
No half on childcare, have a baby with them and you
loose
There are things that monetary support can't buy
Like bedtime stories, first day of school, bonds and
memories that only emotional support can provide
How do you answer a child that asks what does my father
look like?
How did we go from father's tearing open the skies
To a growing number who depart before ever saying hi
The forecast calls for rain, just look at the skies.

Dixie Land

Old Dixie South is burning again

Like James Meredith trying to get his registration back

in.

Except this is not 1962 and there will not be any troops

going back in.

But the truth is rattling

Exposing the souls that nourish our very existence

And it doesn't take much digging

Because hate can never stay hidden

And the candidates I don't care to debate

The real issue at hand is why Louisiana still thinks like an

enslaved state

Mona Lisa

He paints.
I peered deep into his eyes and watched his soul paint
Washing the brush in his tears and dipping it back in his
pain
With each stroke and glide he painted his heartbreak
And as I watched there appeared her face
She was his Mona Lisa
Far from perfect and yet still so beautiful
Her soul could do no wrong; it was her flesh that was
sinful
She swore she loved him and no other
And since she tells no lies he blames God when she loves
another
He's been crying for days and painting for weeks
Praying for a break, using Ambien to sleep
Her face forever embedded in his memory
And I watch as he paints
Everyday a tormented man

Who Are These Faces?

Do this in remembrance of me.
Do this in remembrance of me.
Pass the chalice please.
They're screaming running on top of blood soaked
grounds
chanting
FOOD NOT BOMBS!
I am haunted by her face. Agony painted upon her skin.
Eyes wide like her soul can't take in this panoramic view
of sin.
All she can do is lay on the ground holding her son's
hand.
SCREAMING
While his father rocks his lifeless body, hand covering the
hole from which his brain is seeping.
I do not understand Swahili, but I know every time that
mother opened her mouth it was to God she was speak-
ing.
We've seen their faces on Fox News, CNN, and MSNBC
Every time we log in their tragedies fill our newsfeed

But who are these faces?

A 911 dispatcher in Sanford, Fl receives a call.

"This guy looks like he is up to no good."

I guess in today's society you're a menace if you're a black

man wearing a hood.

Because Trayvon was guilty before charged; killed before

convicted

Catapulting the

good/ bad,

right/wrong,

black/white

of our judicial system

into a media courtroom where we saw their faces.

Their faces filled both sides of the street

Happy anxious faces awaiting the sound of runners feet.

And in an instance happiness was replaced by fear.

Screams and cries, no longer cheers.

Mass confusion because death is not welcomed here!

And those were the faces of children

the faces of men and women

Black, white faces,

red, yellow faces,

clay colored faces

Who are these faces?

We are these faces

These Assalamu Alaykum faces

These pamoja tutashinda faces

These celebrer la vie faces

These dios es amor faces

These in frieden leben faces

We are these faces

It is time we learn to love our faces.

Judy's Daughter

My mother's name is Angela, but this poem isn't
 dedicated to her
Or to one of my favorites
No, I didn't write this for Angela Davis
But instead for Angela
Angela in Atlanta
No, not the dancer
But the daughter of Judy, the mother of Shay
This poem is for Angela who went missing on the eve of
my birthday
Whose worth
Is now being determined by her work
"There for, but by the grace of God goes I"
Only circumstances separates us from every person who
walks this earth.
And who are we to judge anyways when we are the ones
who created this thing called "twerk"
A nation fixated on lust
Arch your back girl, stick out your bust
Make your ass clap; all the ballers show love
When our Queens turn up missing the blame is on us

I write this for Angela because her life was stolen before
she had the chance to even grow
We are haste to judge the things we see, but quick to
forget there is a past for every pew, seat filled in our
churches front rows
The only difference is the luxury of time
Because if given enough anything lost can again be found
I write this for Angela because we owe her an apology
You see monsters can only grow when we allow them to
eat.
And there are predators out there that we continue to
feed.
Little broken boys that never grow into Kings
Living out some rap lies believing they are entitled to
everything
Bang, bang take mentality.
We blast this shit in our clubs so don't get mad at me.
I'm just the messenger.... standing 4'11 like Angela, but
somebody has to speak
The truth
Or next week it could be me or you
And don't be foolish to think this is exclusive to girls who
frequent the "Champagne Room"
I write this for Angela, I write this for Shay

I write this for Judy and all of the beautiful souls we have lost along the way.
How many wake up calls does it really take, until we are truly up and awake?

Rest Peacefully Angela Rabotte

Micaela Mone'

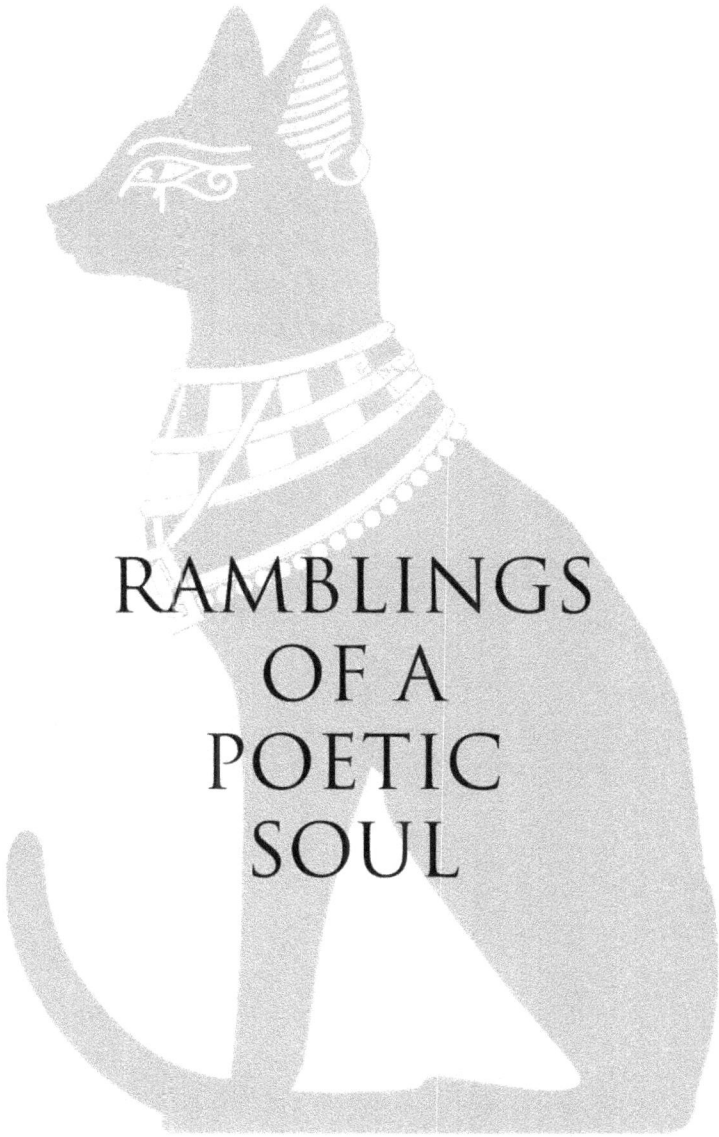

RAMBLINGS
OF A
POETIC
SOUL

Perhaps my addiction is sadness
I'm addicted to the tears, shouting & madness
Perhaps my obsession is loneliness
So I seek out the ones that will loan me it
Perhaps my illness is bitterness
Swallowing pills
fighting not to regurgitate
forgiveness
Perhaps my enemy lives in me
And I'm standing between lines bombing myself
innerly

From behind a window I witness poverty
Helpless eyes that don't see a way out
Grime on wailing angels
Broke is all they know
From their pocketbooks to their souls
But I see hope and it is beautiful

Micaela Mone'

I found you floating in a river like Moses
Treated you like royalty, but your vision remained out of
focus
And my only hope is
one day you will wear your crown.

Sometimes I feel like I'm drowning on dry lands
Reaching for God with slippery hands
Wet from tears that never dry
Isn't this face a beautiful disguise?
Don't hand me Kleenexs I'll be alright
But if you have a prayer to spare please lift me high
I'm drowning on dry lands
But even through these tears His grip is tight on my hands.

For years I wondered what it would feel like
Nights upon nights I prayed
Nothing grand.
It was quiet.
For a moment I worried that something was terribly
wrong with me
Then I realized that peace is still and this is what it feels
like not to cry.

I'm afraid to go to sleep
because I'll see you in my dreams.
I don't want to stay awake
Because these memories won't go away.

Alice no wonderland.

Is it six yet?

My kettle is whistling, but the table's not set.

Mad Hatter is coming, to hell with the dishes

Blue pill, red pill

both idle wishes

Take them both

Swallow fast and don't choke

I'm neither here nor there; tucked in between a poem,

riddle, and a quote.

I Am

Even Superwoman has her bad days
But she flies just the same with a torn cape
She hides her tears behind a happy face
Because who wants to see a broken hero anyways

I just want to lay down in my notebook and cover myself in its sheets.
I want to lay my head down on my words and dream of them while I sleep.
If ever the day should come that I have to leave just open my notebook and there I shall be.

How vain are we that our lips speak only of the beauty
of the flower and not of its birth?
That our eyes see only the color of its petals and not the
supplier of its strength buried beneath the dirt.
How vain are we?
How selfish are we to bask in the warmness of the sun
like it is our right?
And forget quickly of her presence as soon as it is night.
How selfish are we?

Trying to right my wrongs
has me up late nights writing poems.
Confessionals without a priest.
Tossing Hail Mary's every time my pen release.

I do not want to be touched physically so please no hands allowed.
I only want to be touched mentally
That's how intellects become aroused.

Let's exchange negatives
And expose them to our inner lights
To develop something positive
Would that be alright?
Film strips
Filled with soul trips
Let's eclipse
Show me the places where only my love can fit

.

I want love like a wide open field that the wind kisses, sun adores, the rain showers, and the stars gaze nightly in awe of its beauty.

I know what it is like to cry more than to smile;
to have tears dance upon my eyelids daring to fall.
Trying my damndest not to blink or breathe at all
because the sting of pain is much too familiar.
And I'm simply tired of visiting.
I know what it is like to cry.

*I spend late nights searching for something I have
already found.
This is madness.
I walk with a crow fastened to my chest.
This is blackness.
Each peck chipping at the cage where a silly heart rests.
And I let this
Because my heart fails me each time.
There's no need to salvage.*

Micaela Mone'

I am a vessel
I have been both full and empty
Waiting
gestation periods
Until my soul dilates;
ready to deliver
I am a vessel.

She says she wants something magical, but the problem
with magic is
once it abracadabra it always disappears
Exposing smoking mirrors yes all that mist clears.
Forcing you to taste the confirmations of your own
worst fears.
That magic is just an illusion.

Today I wore the tears of a little boy who found out his
superhero wasn't real.
Face pressed against mine, his tears became mine and
every stab of disappointment I did feel.

Like a slave receiving 100 lashes
my body is here, but my mind is far away .
I have peace.
I have freedom.
I'll rise again in the morning.

Every now and then my heart beats funny.
Probably from the fact that stress keeps coming.
Call me Jesse Owens because I can't stop running.
Skip if you may just don't stop drumming.

You're searching for a distraction because you don't
want to think for too long
Because your thought process has a tendency to roam
And you don't want to remember
No anything but remember
So you're searching for a feeling
because it's too painful when memories simmer
Turn the fire all the way down
Lights low, anything to keep those memories from
coming back around
In search of a distraction purposely leaving your heart
in lost and found

She had eyes like Judas, but I still fed her well.
Never a deaf ear I knew she never wished me well.
So I keep a close watch, never kiss and tell.
My grand pop was right not all demons stay in hell.

And maybe I over think
over analyze, over feel.
Maybe I remember too well to ever heal.
Then again, what exactly is it that I feel?

We live in an aesthetic world.
Ass shots and Botox.
Forget what your soul looks like.
What your soul looks like?
Yea, what your soul looks like.

METHUSELAH

Some nights, after I leave the sheddings of my day at the foot of my bed, I lay deep within my thoughts. A million thoughts waiting in my mind to be explored and pondered upon. A million more thoughts to be conceived. And sometimes I think of you.

Bird

I knew he was a bird; I had kissed his kind before

Blood still on my lips from the last peck

Scapular in my back pocket I can't help but to help

Mother Teresa Novena and I'm not even Catholic

I must have been baptized in irony because that's all I see

Wade in Typhoon waters foreseeing the grief

But that's just me

And I sang along

Every lyric, every moan

Strumming his feathers, sleeping on his wings

Rising in the morning to the whispers of his dreams

And then listening closely to the percussions of his chest

Memorizing every beat before he left

Because I knew he was a bird and was born to be free

And I was his temporary savior, placing love at his altar

replenishing him before he would leave

I let him feast

Because I know even birds become weak.

Fiji

My bags have been packed forever and earlier today I
grabbed them and ran
Drove to Houston and boarded a plane
13 hours later I'm standing here with sand beneath my
feet
And you in front of me
We always clowned about how it was suppose to be
And this is it.
I no longer have to replay your heart beat
Because every night it will sing me to sleep
We left our phones behind, disconnected from the world
No distractions because time is precious and we have so
much to explore
I write you poetry; you read me books
I lost count on how many times we came...
Came to the conclusion that forever wasn't long enough
And like Methuselah not even 13 billion years would be
long enough to give you all of my love.
So just cover me now
Don't let the sun catch us
"Mommy, Mommy, I'm thirsty."
Wait how did I get here

I Am

Damn I was dreaming again because you're not here
Not here with me
And this is not Fiji
Four in the morning dilemma

Bittersweet

Bittersweet
That's why I avoid love songs because they only remind
me of all the moments I will never share with you
Secretly I mourn the death of a love that I will never bear
with you
So like Jesus I walk to my cross.... sacrificing my heart
see that's how much I care for you
Friendship is the only way I can always be there for you
Bittersweet
Because in truth we're both like Egyptian Gods
Causing eclipses every time we cross each other in the
skies
And since we're all made from star dust
Maybe we collided billions of years ago
Considering I'm always late may explain why our light
travelled so slow
Because no matter how impossible I swear I knew you
before
Bittersweet
This life is like a garden; at least we got to see the flower
even if we can't watch it grow
At this moment I'm at a standstill in awe of your

presence.....

North Star

On an average day I imagine a thousand thoughts
speeding inside of my head like shooting stars in a galaxy.
Some of them slowing for me to ponder upon; streaking
their light against my brain.
And then there's you.
Never rising or setting just constant like the North Star as
I spin on my axis.

Full Moon

The moon is full tonight

That is how I wish to be

And you are endless like the sky, so can you please hold
me?

Surrounded by the stars we can be

Naked

No reservations

Souls wrapped in constellations

Let me inside

My lips against your flaws

Waves spilling over your walls

Can I fill you?

Fill the holes they left behind

Lay with the thoughts inside of your mind

The moon is full tonight.

Love Astronomy

They collided like two stars from different galaxies
An astrophysical rarity
Conceiving a Blue Star
Their love was a supernova phenomenon but was never
meant to be
It grew big
It grew fast
Quickly replaced by another star that we now see
Shined bright and dimmed out
That was their love's astronomy

Transit of Venus

Just a dot

I was a mere dot kissing your perimeter

Awakened by your flames

Spinning retrograde as we danced across the horizon

A slow, sensuous dance reserved for only lovers

And we

We were like Egyptian Gods

With every touch we were eclipsing

Momentarily forgetting

That this was just a transit

A crossing of paths

Hello

Good bye

Venus only dances with the Sun when all three planets

are aligned

Because of this I am certain we won't dance again this

lifetime.

Micaela Mone'

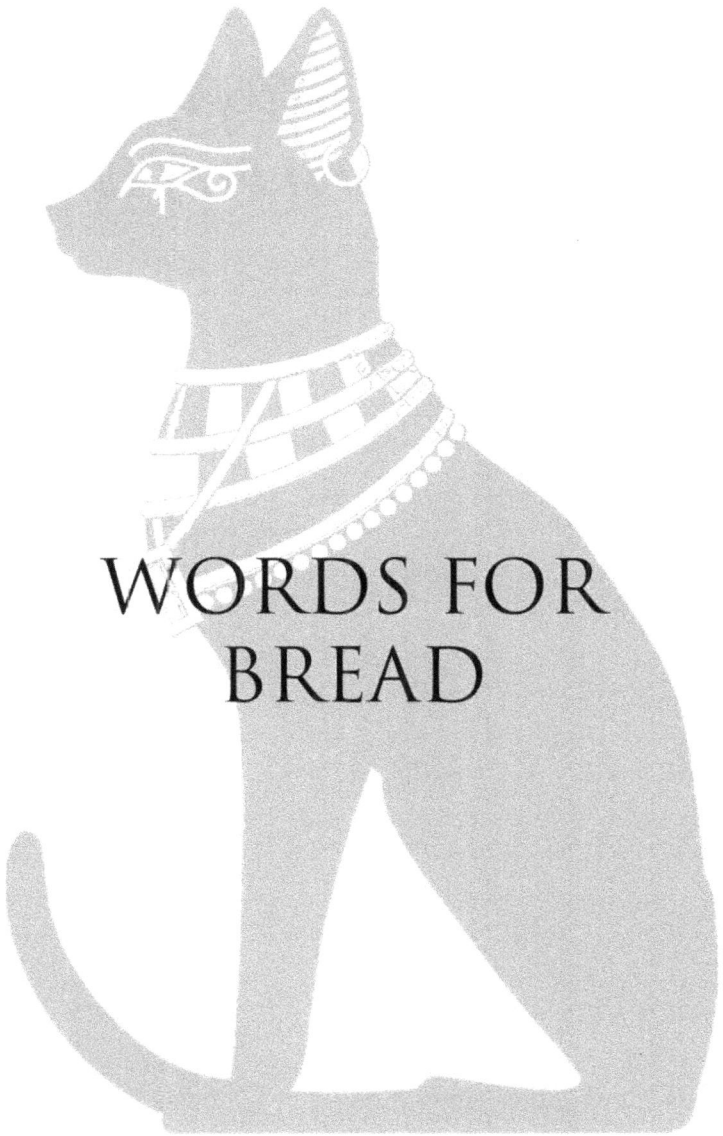

WORDS FOR
BREAD

It's always in retrospect I see the dagger in my own hand.

sometimes walking away from
the battle wins the war.

When the skies are dark and my walls are closing; my thoughts are loud and these lines are posed.

Is it mad of me to wander in my thoughts alone? To seek solace in my silence. Is it terribly wrong?

In the process of discovering him I lost myself thus no discoveries were made only more explorations.

The most self destructive thing a fatherless woman can do is to search for a daddy. She'll miss him every time.

I want to indulge in a conversation so deep that remnants of your soul are left upon my lips.

Fear is a gateway drug that can cause anxiety, self doubt, and ultimately self destruction. It has the ability to hold you captive if you allow it to. Do not allow fear to keep you from living the life you deserve. Do not allow fear to rob you of your dreams. Be present in the now.
Be Fearless!

We all have demons, some of us just run faster. We all have blessings, but some of us just walk pass them.

The worst thing for a girl to be is naive. The big bad wolf ventures beyond the woods of grandmother's house. Quite often the wolf walks beside us.

No matter how many storms I see or tears I wipe away a poem somehow rises in me.

The road divides somewhere between good and evil, erasing trails of good intentions. The road divides somewhere between good and evil.

Everyone will not see your vision. You will cross paths with people who will try to convince you that your dream is not worth pursuing. Pursue it anyways! It is better to try and fail than to lay in a "regret filled coffin". Dream big, fight hard, and never tap out!

If you're not careful you will wander in the wilderness convinced you're still in Egypt. Freedom or bondage begins in the mind.

Your actions and what you want have to be on one accord in order to see true progress. Every fiber of your being must be in agreement.

Everyone has a back story. You have to make sure it doesn't become your entire story.

I'm far from perfect.
I stopped burying my flaws because sometimes they resurface.

How many hours have I wasted?
Wasted wondering how I ended
up here. Waking up many nights
lost because this is not the bed I
imagined I would be sleeping in.
Lost and searching for the one I
belong in.

Sometimes you have to detox from the people around you. They are a part of the things we consume daily and can inadvertently be toxic.

Be cautious of the thoughts you entertain in your head. The longer you fancy them the stronger they will grow. Manifestation is real.

Wolves may disguise themselves in sheep's wool, but they can never hide their teeth! Know the wolves in your life and when they begin knocking, leave them at the door!

A soldier doesn't go to boot camp because they like it; they go because they need the training. Storms are our boot camps. It's up to us to come out stronger.

Even when I'm sinking my head
is above water.
I'm a Giant!
Nothing less than the King's
daughter
I'm a Giant!

Sometimes we hold onto things so tight that we fail to realize nothing is in our grip. Closed hands can't receive. Know what you're holding! Don't miss your blessing because your hands were closed, holding onto nothing.

Micaela Mone'

God will make your enemies your footstool, but it is up to you to be Christ like and pull them back up.

148

I Am

Dating is like fishing. You can't expect to catch salmon if you're fishing in muddy waters. Don't get mad at the mudfish when you catch him. It is not his fault he's a mudfish, it is your fault for fishing in dirty waters.

Every fighter gets tired, but a winner never stops swinging! I refuse to tap out!

If it comes easy I don't want it! Let me fight for it, cry tears over it, and struggle during my climb to the top. Adversity will remind me to never take it for granted. Easy come, easy go! It's the struggle that teaches you to fight.

In my silence I speak my loudest. From my corner I shout onto paper. The truth is not always beautiful so I rather you see it than to be told.

Inside of me I have the soul of an old bayou lady that rocks on her porch while sipping lemonade telling her truth to passer byers.

I'll fight for you even when there's no fight left in you. I'll block for you when your back is against the wall and you can't break through. I'll pray for you the words that your soul cries inside. I'll wait with you through that midnight hour until sunrise.

People that find delight in another person's faults are simply trying to distract themselves from their own faults. Misery loves company.

Never expect people to be anything other than who they are. A snake will never be a butterfly no matter how much skin it sheds. The same applies to people. Be cautious and use your good sense because there are people amongst us that make Judas look like a saint.

Once again I've slipped down the rabbits hole. I wonder if they'll miss me when the tea is served?

I stood in front of a mirror and saw all of my weaknesses, but instead chose to tell my reflection about my strengths.

There came a time in my life when I was tired of the chaos. I could no longer stomach the drama so I decided to erase it. And upon the space where a fragment once filled I wrote a declaration. I am free!

Just beneath the surface of my pain I find hope. It is there that words wait for me to write them on paper. Heartbreak is poetry to me.

Creating art can be liken to a woman in labor. Sometimes the worst pain in your life delivers your most beautiful creation.

one day I will dream upon dry
pillows.

I AM

I Am

Daily I am rising from my ashes

Because I am the child that was rejected

Helpless

Molested

Depression left me restless

Reckless

I felt this.

I am more than the chains that tried to keep me shackled

Stronger than the giants that I daily have to wrestle

I am a mother that sacrifices

Providing despite prices

Crisis

I fight it

Guilt, I can't hide it.

My nights are sleepless

But the lack of time keeps me tireless

I am a swimmer in an ocean that is never quiet

I was born with my fist raised so when a Tsunami appears

I just ride it.

I am the hero that prays for a miracle

I may not be Criss Angel, but I can turn my pain into

something lyrical

I am the very words that I write

My soul is dipped in ink

I am proof that after every dark night the sun does rise

I am my mother's daughter

I am the lifeline of my father

I am a forgiver learning how to forgive

I am a dreamer desperately trying to make them real

A builder

The essence of a giver

I am wombman

The power of my foremothers lays in my hands

I am a poet, a lover, a survivor, and a warrior

I am beautiful, worthy, forgiven, and loved

I am unashamed of my scars

I am proud of my heart

My imperfections are mine and I will not hide them away

I am a scholar learning lessons day by day

I am rising.

I am surviving.

I am still here.

About the Author

Micaela Mone' is a poet from Eunice, Louisiana. Writing along with acting has been her passion since she was a child. She believes that everyone has a story and every story deserves to be told. Poetry is her story. She writes with transparency in hopes of speaking to souls. Her ultimate goals are to give hope to the hopeless, love to the broken, and peace to the restless. Currently, she is pursuing a degree in Nursing and working on the release of her first children's book "My Name is Queen". Micaela has many hats and titles, but she loves nothing more than being a mother to her three kids. "I Am" is her second published book of poetry. Her previous book of poetry, "Behind Closed Eyes", is available online.

Children's Book Coming Soon!

"My Name is Queen"

Micaela Mone'
Nekeeta Guillory

www.ingramcontent.com/pod-product-compliance
Lightning Source LLC
Chambersburg PA
CBHW020857090426
42736CB00008B/411